T0194098

HOPE

How Faith Carried Me
Through My Darkest Hours

Mercedes E Wilson

WESTBOW
PRESS*
A DIVISION OF THOMAS NELSON
& ZONDERVAN

Copy editors: Colleen O'Hara, Helen Rosca

Interior Image Credit: Ally Spongr

All scripture quotations marked are from https://www.biblegateway.com

Scripture quotations marked MSG are taken from THE MESSAGE, copyright © 1993, 1994, 1995, 1996, 2000, 2001, 2002 by Eugene H. Peterson. Used by permission of NavPress. All rights reserved. Represented by Tyndale House Publishers, Inc.

Scripture quotations marked (AMP) are taken from the Amplified Bible, Copyright © 1954, 1958, 1962, 1964, 1965, 1987 by The Lockman Foundation. Used by permission.

Scripture taken from the King James Version of the Bible.

This book is a work of non-fiction. Unless otherwise noted, the author and the publisher make no explicit guarantees as to the accuracy of the information contained in this book and in some cases, names of people and places have been altered to protect their privacy. WestBow Press books may be ordered through booksellers or by contacting:

WestBow Press
A Division of Thomas Nelson & Zondervan
1663 Liberty Drive
Bloomington, IN 47403
www.westbowpress.com
1 (866) 928-1240

Because of the dynamic nature of the Internet, any web addresses or links contained in this book may have changed since publication and may no longer be valid. The views expressed in this work are solely those of the author and do not necessarily reflect the views of the publisher, and the publisher hereby disclaims any responsibility for them.

Any people depicted in stock imagery provided by Getty Images are models, and such images are being used for illustrative purposes only.
Certain stock imagery © Getty Images.

ISBN: 978-1-9736-1808-9 (sc)
ISBN: 978-1-9736-1807-2 (hc)
ISBN: 978-1-9736-1809-6 (e)

Library of Congress Control Number: 2018901615

Print information available on the last page.

WestBow Press rev. date: 02/28/2018

Mercedes Wilson's faith shines through her words, and gives readers a true sense of hope. Her words are almost like prayers, even psalms. Her personal story of cancer and recovery is moving; but more so is the gripping drama of life barging in: her anguish when her young son sees her without her wig is so raw that it almost takes one's breath away. But then she swallows hard and answers him to calm his fear, and his acceptance in turn helps her. What a wonderful testimony to a mother's love and what a beautiful life moment!
—Mary R. Arno, author of Thanksgiving

It's truly inspirational, encouraging, thought provoking, and hands down one of the most authentic forms of spiritual transparency I have experienced on paper. This book is a must read for those who are gripped by feelings of hopelessness and discouragement. You will be blessed!
—First Lady Tiffany Gilbert, Kingdom Restoration Christian Center-KRCC

Compelling, endearing, and written with pure and genuine emotion. Readers will be inspired by Wilson and her journey into self-discovery by learning to forgive herself and others through spirituality. A must read for anyone that needs a reminder that they are not alone in the trials and tribulations that life offers and that there is always hope
—Sandra Lahrache, Founder of The Teal Project

DEDICATIONS

My husband James, my love, my protector, my friend, you are a big reason why writing this book is possible. You encouraged me to start writing when I told you my vision, took care of our kids when I needed some time away, and pushed me when I was afraid of actually taking steps to make this book happen. So many times, you told me how proud of me you were and to just keep going! Thank you for your excitement to see this come to pass. I love you.

To all of my children, you are the reasons that I work so hard at everything that I do. I could not be any more proud of you all. Always be who you are without apologizing. I will always love you!

To my aunt Cynthia and uncle David, thank you for opening up your doors in my greatest time of need. Uncle David, you always said that what I was experiencing as a teenager was making me stronger and you were right! I love you both with all of my heart! Thank you to their children, my cousins, for opening up your lives and allowing me to be a part of yours. To the same cousins, thank you for encouraging me to get this book done.

To my parents, I love you. This journey has taught all of us what real love looks like. Thank you both for having the courage to love again. We are all wiser and stronger because of our willingness to love through the tough times.

To my baby sister, thank you for having my niece! I love you Gianna! Thank you for recognizing that although tough at times, that a sisters' bond is everlasting. I love you very much and I am very proud of the woman that you have become.

Stephanie, Helen, and Ethel, my best friends! Thank you all for your undying love. Love is an action word and you ladies show it every day. Very few people are able to be transparent with others and still remain friends. I love you all.

To my in-laws, thank you for all of your love and undying support. Our relationships mean a lot to me.

To my mentors and friends,(there's too many to name), thank you for being there for me and having my back when I said I was going to write a book. You all inspire me. Thank you all for your sound counsel. I am who I am because of you all.

To my lawyer Crystal J. Rodriguez, Esq, and my branding coach Carmel Carson, thank you both for being here to give me wise counsel through this process. I appreciate what you both do in order to help women succeed at their passion!

CONTENTS

FOREWORD

"Hope"
By:
Pastor J. Anthony Gilbert

I have heard it said that you cannot bypass process to get to progress. Mercedes Wilson and the journey she has travelled is the personification of this reality.

I have known Mercedes for 18 years and it has been a joy to see the prophetic negatives develop into the full color photo of destiny through the darkroom of her journey. Throughout her process I have witnessed her ups, downs, successes, and failures. I have rejoiced with her in times of rejoicing and wept with her in times of mourning. The one thing that has been a constant reality about her life, is her steadfastness with the Lord.

When you walk with someone for this amount of time, it is impossible to not witness the intrinsic essence and core of who they are. I remember when I first met her and she started attending the church that I was pastoring. The first thing I remember about her was the genuineness of her heart and desire to please the Lord.

As many know and can attest that when we start on this journey we are usually so excited about all of the dreams and possibilities that life has out in front of us that seem to be right around the corner. We become so excited about obtaining that degree, getting married, having a family, starting a business or a ministry, and maybe one day reaching a certain socioeconomic status. I believe God has a sense of humor, in the fact that, He has a way of showing us the brilliance of our destiny while omitting the detours that devastate us on the way to our destination. It does not seem like it at the time but God uses all of these devastations to create in us the character needed to carry the dream He has placed in our hearts and on our lives. While we are in the process it seems like all hope is gone and that we will never come out of where we are.

In this book Mercedes opens up and shows us the devastations that can happen on our journey and the pain that it can cause, while giving us hope that God is in control and at work in us and around us in the process. Through the raw disclosure of her life's process you sense the feelings of her pain through childhood abuse, betrayal, divorce, and the pain of miscarriage. You also see and experience the triumph from her trials, the power from her pain, and the resurrection from the ashes of her past. No matter how difficult it may seem, by the grace and power of God, He uses what the devil means for evil and turns it around for our good. You will leave off reading this book saying to yourself, "If God can do it for her, surely He can do it for me!".

Anyone that has a dream that has gone through or going through abuse, hurt, pain, or feelings of loneliness should read this book. Mercedes shows us that no matter how deep the pain, there is healing, no matter how dark the tunnel there is light, no matter the depths of your despair, In Christ, there is HOPE.

PREFACE

Since my childhood, I have told my innermost thoughts to God. Sometimes they were through song and sometimes they were hidden tears. I knew that God kept account of every tear I shed and would one day allow me to make the tears into something that helped others. This book is my love letter to God and His goodness, along with my pains that were shared with Him. This book is also proof that while you can be a product of your experiences growing up, that there's still nothing too great for God. All of us were put here for a reason, and our experiences, whether good or bad, can be turned around for our good. My experiences wouldn't be triumphs without God. There's no way that I could have formulated my life to be what it is today.

My desire is that this book gives you a new perspective and approach to the something that God wants all of us to have ... HOPE. Hope is something that has to be worked for. The word hope may sound extravagant and grand, but unless intentionally sought, it can be hard to acquire. Throughout the book there are pages to write down some things that are on your mind. Take advantage of these pages, allow yourself to go to the hard places and then release them to God. There's so much freedom in doing this.

We have been sold the false impression that this thing called life is supposed to be easy. Without the help of the Holy Spirit, I would not have made it. Most people only know of my battle with breast cancer; however, there is so much more to my story. This is my testimony, I hope you are inspired.

"And not only so, but we glory in tribulations also; knowing that tribulation worth patience; And patience, experience; and experience, hope" Romans 5:3-4;KJV

1

HOPE DEFERRED

Every Easter and Christmas, my parents had us dressed to impress! I am talking about beautiful dresses, stockings, and the shiny shoes that had the little click when we walked. I used to act like a model on a runway for weeks after these services, just to hear my shoes click. My family didn't go to church often outside of these two holidays. When I got older, someone described us as being "Chreasters" because we only went on Christmas and Easter. That gave me a good chuckle.

To my sister and I, my parents were the best folks ever. My mom was the main disciplinarian because she stayed home with us. My father worked a lot, so when he was home, he spoiled us. I remember my mother throwing a fit because he came home one day and handed me a one-hundred dollar bill for my birthday. I was very young at the time, so she thought this was crazy! My father and I both laughed at her because there was no way I was giving it back—nor would my father make me.

My sister and I loved the summers! My father had a deep love for nice cars, so he would take my sister and I to a park so we could play all day while he cleaned his car. Sometimes we would begin to hear music playing as friends and family would fill the park. What would start out as a day at the park could end up being a family reunion at times.

My baby sister and I were very close, except for the one time that she told on me for sneaking outside on the back porch and smoking my mother's cigarettes! She was my sidekick and was pretty cool to be around. Because we were only two years apart, playing together came easy.

I was born with singing in my blood, so I used to force everyone to sing songs with me. In my mind, I was going to be the next Whitney Houston, so everyone was forced to hear me sing her songs all day long My father and I used to sing together often, and I would force my sister to be a background singer. Most children played outside for fun. Me? I sang.

Just like most other children, I witnessed my parents arguing a few times. What couples don't? There was a particular argument that I knew the tone was different, though, and this argument came as a result of my mother and me finding odd jewelry and clothing while cleaning one weekend. I could tell by the look on her face that none of the items we found belonged to her. There was a pit in my stomach because even though she didn't say another word, I knew something was about to happen—and it felt like it was partly my fault. When I heard my parents arguing, all that I could think was, *What did I do?*

My sister and I then experienced what was known to everyone as a very nasty and public divorce. When it came time to choose who we wanted to live with, we chose opposite households. I can't even describe what was going on in my young mind after not only losing what I saw as a dynamic family, but also losing my baby sister to something that we could do nothing about.

When a child experiences a divorce of the two people who make up their world, multiple things happen on the inside, and unfortunately uncertainty, insecurity, and confusion become deep-rooted pains. Young people have the unique ability to fault themselves for a divorce.

My decision to live with my mother clearly hurt my father because our communication stopped entirely for years. He and my sister went on with their lives, and we went on with ours. Visits with my sister were tense. I felt like I no longer knew her, but the reality was we both thought that we were expressing our love through. That breech in our sisterly bond followed us for years to come.

My young life became all about finding validation for my existence. I just needed someone to do something with this hurt that was on the inside. My sources of relief were music and writing. I started writing poems that described my pain. I got rid of a lot of them for fear of someone finding them and learning of my innermost, sometimes scary, thoughts.

A young person's life can be forever effected by a sexual predator that people don't give a second thought to. Someone that no one among your life circle might realize is capable of such tremendous harm. A delivery man, a coach who crosses the line, the harmless neighbor next door ... no one among my family or friends knew the identity of my abuser. We have all seen the television episodes that show unimaginable things happening to ruin the innocence of a child. These types of acts are something that I could never understand, but it was my reality. I was made to put my hand down his pants, and the same was done to me. I was asked to get undressed and walk in front of him, to kiss this adult as if I were one myself. Disgusting is an understatement of what I experienced. I needed a hero—a protector—and it seemed as though I was all alone. I often daydreamed of someone saving me.

These experiences changed the very core of who I was. I had always been an outgoing child (I had the nickname of Motor Mouth Mercedes), but after this I became depressed and all I wanted to do was sleep.

When I was about thirteen years old, I met a woman named Melissa, who gave me something positive in my life to focus on. She saw something in me. She encouraged me to make the merit roll in school and promised to take me out for lunch or dinner as an incentive. I worked hard to hit merit roll and once I did we went to eat (Anyone that knows me knows that I love great food and company)! Spending time with her taught me a few things, one of them being her faith. She had a past—a deep, dark past—and she shared with me how she was forgiven by God. When she told me her story, something connected with me. That deep-rooted pain that I could not describe before finally had a voice.

She invited me to church with her, and when I walked in I remember seeing a woman pastor and she was full of fire as she preached. Near the end of service, I had no clue what drew me to the altar, but when I got there, all I could do was fall to my knees. For the first time in a long time in my short life, I felt *hope*. I felt understood in a way that validated my

3

existence. I was no longer rejected in this setting, and the pain that I felt was understood.

I didn't stand up from the altar a renewed and changed young lady; rather, I stood up with the strength for the journey.

Starting that journey of faith gave me the courage to say something about the abuse. I didn't know how to show my emotions and pain. My mother's perception was that I was an unruly teenager, and after much discussion with her, it was decided that I would go live with my aunt and uncle.

My aunt and uncle were very patient and sensitive to what I had just gone through. I had the chance to see great relationships, along with getting a glimpse of having a positive male role model. I had lost so much weight at this point (due to stress and not eating) that I was in a size zero!

Once my family came to my rescue, I tried to live what I considered to be a "normal" life, but the damage was already done. Until I went off to college, my family did what they could to show me stability. I had so many displaced emotions and thoughts, so being in a normal setting was abnormal to me. Even with all of this positivity around me, I had deep rejection and abandonment issues.

One thing that was very evident from all of my experiences was that I had formed a habit of running, in my mind, to deal with the pain. To keep my sanity, I had become accustomed to creating false realities. While in school I focused on what was important to me, which was trying my best so I could get away when it came time for college.

In my running, I chose to get married at the age of eighteen. I was looking for a knight in shining armor to take me away from all of my pain, and I was determined to live the opposite of what I had known. I said that I would stay away and raise my children to know security, unconditional love, and stability. I hoped to be a good mother, wife, and friend.

The thing about running from your past into your future is that success doesn't happen that way. While on the journey to being a better you, you have to change your mindset and allow time to heal from things before pursuing something else. I thought that I would be different than every other woman who tried to run from her past into her future; I had it mapped out, and I just knew my way would work.

Even with all of the pain that I felt, there was always this thing on the inside of me that told me to hold on....that more was to come. I held on to that with all that I had-Mercedes Wilson

2

BROKEN

I didn't see many healthy examples of relationships. I don't know if I was a nosy child or if the people around me had inappropriate conversations, but I heard a lot. I heard talks about affairs and talks of mistresses, and several times over my childhood witnessed women getting beaten by their spouses. I couldn't stop thinking about those experiences for years to come. As a result of what I witnessed as a child, men had very low stock in my mind.

Imagine any young woman experiencing this degree of dysfunction in relationships thinking she is mature enough to get married at 18 years old. I was told several times not to do it, that I would end up a statistic and the numbers were against us. I was told "You came from a broken home so that makes your chances of failure even higher". I remember seeing my wedding attendees crying and wondering if they were tears of joy or tears as a result of thinking *"she is making a mistake"*.

I got pregnant at 19 years old, and when my son was born my heart melted. He had piercing ocean blue eyes, a perfect nose. I loved just grabbing his tiny little fingers, toes and examining them. He was just fascinating to me. I watched him blink and smile in amazement. Is this what my parents felt like when I was born? Did they feel the joy of seeing life come from them like I did? Did they look at me in amazement and make a vow to always make sure I was safe? My life was forever changed. I loved having a family and I felt that I had arrived!

No relationship is perfect, this includes everything from friendships to marriage. During my marriage, major issues were on the list to be dealt with and like so many other couples, counseling was in order. I could hear my family now. "See! This is why you should have waited to get married, we told you that you were too young, you haven't lived any of your life yet and now you have to deal with this!"

We decided to try for another child shortly after my son was born. I had just finished up my Associates degree, started on my Bachelor's, and was very excited about that, but still wanted to grow my family. Since I was going to school the non-traditional way (online) it was doable in my mind. I wanted my family!

I got pregnant, but unfortunately, I experienced my first of my two miscarriages. I knew something was wrong, I just had the feeling, but it didn't stop me from feeling the pain of losing a baby. I chose to have a D and C (Dilation and Curettage) rather than wait it out and cried for days. I felt as though my body was defective. I felt as though I failed my family, but within 6 weeks I was pregnant again and then came my baby girl!

I really prayed for her. My exact prayer to God when I found out that I was pregnant was "please give me a girl that I can show how to be a woman". I wanted a chance at raising a confident young woman, the one I felt I never was. My girl was born!

She came out with the same big eyes as my son, except hers were a beautiful brown. She was my smiley baby. She was also my greedy baby, she loved to eat! I was so complete; my heart was complete, my life was complete.

That feeling of being complete was short lived because my first marriage ended in divorce right after I had to file bankruptcy. Guess what was included in that bankruptcy? My first home. The home that I had for so long dreamed about and worked so hard for. Gone.

Hurt and embarrassed can't even begin to touch my true feelings after these experiences. Everyone hears the stories about the house with the white picket fence and the dog, right? No one ever talks about what really happens in life, that everything takes work. You are also not told that even if you work hard, sometimes, undesirable things still happen.

A couple years later I went to visit a friend that lived near my first house. The home was still vacant and open, it was just the way I left it. I went into the house and immediately the memories overtook me.

My first home had three bedrooms, two bathrooms, and a mudroom! I was told so many times when my family visited my house that "black people don't have mudrooms" LOL. I walked in that mudroom and remembered how I took so much pride in decorating it. I loved putting down the flooring and painting, finding the right curtains, and setting up the decor. I walked through my kitchen and recalled how excited I was that I had an island with a dishwasher installed in it. I had so many memories of cooking meals in that kitchen. I loved looking out of my back window at the shed and watching the train behind my house go by.

My deck was connected to the kitchen and separated by a beautiful sliding glass door. I loved barbecuing in the summers and passing the food through the serving window to be grilled. My bathroom had His and Her sinks, and it was huge! I also loved taking bubble baths in the tub there. I recalled having Christmas trees in my living room over the years. I loved the windows in this house, because the tree looked so beautiful through the window from the outside. I walked upstairs and into my kids' rooms. I remembered my oldest running through the house yelling, bringing my daughter home from the hospital as a newborn, and getting a cute little puppy we named "Bandit" because he was a white dog with a black patch over one eye.

I took it all in, and then on my way down the beautiful pine stairs I broke down. I sat about halfway down and started screaming. I cried about my failure as a wife, mother, homeowner, daughter-in-law, and example for my kids. How could I have it all, lose it all, and still move forward with my head held high?

I had friends that said over and over again, "Sadie try, try to make your marriage work. You don't want to experience the tearing feeling that comes with divorce". I started journaling shortly before my divorce; and I have to tell you, the pain is real, the tearing even more real. For years, I felt as though I wasn't good enough. A lot of people ask, *why do women stay in relationships when they are unhappy?* I can tell you, for several reasons: low self-esteem, money, stability, wanting to make things work for the kids, or the big one … you have invested so much time in a relationship and you don't want someone else to benefit from your hard work! No relationship can cure YOUR issues! I was extremely worried about how my children would take the news of my divorce. I saw their hearts breaking after I told them the news. My son was about 6 years old, and the way his eyes filled with pain is one thing that I will never forget. Seeing how I experienced a divorce as a child, I knew exactly how my children felt.

Doing the paperwork was the easy part, but it was the pain of literally feeling the tear of a long-term relationship that was hell!

After my divorce, I devoted my time to my job, except when I was trying to fill that void with another relationship! I thought that I was different, that I could move on very quickly and not take time to work on me. I did what so many of us do, move right on and form new soul ties. I was in a whirlwind, and even worse, was I was doing it in anger. I was mad that God allowed childhood abuse, a divorce, for my children to hurt, and for me to hurt like I was. I had been in a relationship at 16, married at 18, first child at 19, and running since I was a little child. I was tired and angry.

My relationships reflected that anger and I used men just like I had been used. I wanted love, but only on my terms. I was on a mission to show God that I had my life under control, because He was obviously too busy. I was doing great with controlling my life, at least that is what I thought until I was diagnosed with stage two breast cancer at the age of 28.

ARE YOU KIDDING ME???

I remember it like it was yesterday. I was in my store preparing for another work day and God spoke to my spirit and said, "Things are about to change". I laughed out loud and said, "I am very busy, I don't have time for anything else". A couple of weeks later doctors performed a biopsy for what they believed was breast cancer. I knew it would come back negative, after all, I was too young, right?

When the doctors confirmed that I had breast cancer it was like the words came out in slow motion. I remember feeling multiple emotions at once…shock, confusion, hurt, anger, then back to shock. How? What next? Did they get me mixed up with someone else? Had to be. When I had to set appointments with other departments to start my process, I knew it was real and that God had it out for me.

I asked if chemo could start in two weeks because I had to get some things settled with my children. Two weeks later, I watched the first dose of chemotherapy go through the tubes and into my port and I took a deep breath and cried. That first treatment was a bear. I remember my sister being there with me and driving me home. I puked as soon as I got settled on my couch. I remember hearing her voice and then I woke up … but it was 3 days later. I went to my first chemo session on a Monday and when I woke up it was a Thursday.

I stared in the mirror at my bald scalp often. Sometimes I was too weak to even cry, but I asked God too many times to count "why me?". At times, the pain from chemotherapy was unbearable. My children had just gone through a divorce, so I chose not to tell them. I wore wigs to try to make myself look as normal as possible. On the weeks that I had chemo my children were away for one week, and that gave me time to recoup and keep life as normal as possible for them.

There was one conversation that I had with my son one evening. I thought that he was asleep and I took off my wig and walked into his room. I was searching for something in my dresser that was in his closet and behind me I heard "Mom you cut your hair?" I was frozen. I replied "Yep, it's a very hot summer so I cut it off". There was what seemed to be a long silence and he said, "I like it!". My heart then returned to my chest and I said, "Thank you baby, now go back to bed".

The reality was I had recently gone to a shop and had them cut the rest of my hair before the chemo took it all. I was told by my doctor that the first chemo session would do nothing to my hair, but after the second treatment, my hair would start to slowly come out. What I didn't expect was for my scalp to be so painful during hair loss. I also didn't expect shaving it off to be as hard as it was. There was silence when I walked into the shop. I cried like a baby the whole time, but when they were finished, the pain from my scalp was no longer there!

The neuropathy from my dying nerve endings got so bad that I had to make hospital visits to help me deal. The palms of my hands, soles of my feet, and finger nails turned black. My skin was beyond dry, I couldn't walk, had muscle pains so bad that I couldn't function, and the insomnia was real!

I had a friend that would come over to my house and practically move in with me to help me cook, clean, grocery shop, anything that I needed. She and a group of friends would look up everything from recipes to symptoms that I would experience before they happened! My cousin found a massage therapist that specialized with cancer patients, and she set me up with appointments to get a massage after each chemo session. We made a schedule for each of my chemotherapy treatments so that different friends or family members could take me every two weeks. I must say, that these ladies were faithful in picking me up, sitting with me throughout my sessions, and bringing me home afterwards! This meant so much to me.

My memory was another area that took a big hit. I struggled to remember things and it had no rhyme or reason to it, I could remember certain things and not others. I forgot what I did yesterday but could tell you everything that happened last week. It was, and still is, incredibly frustrating. On top of all of that, insomnia was my constant companion. No sleep can make one very emotional.

Halfway through my treatments, I found myself crying on my bathroom floor. I was done, wasn't going back for the rest of my chemotherapy, I had decided to just enjoy however long I had left. I called my aunt on the phone and told her I was done. This aunt of mine uses very colorful language and word combinations that will make you scratch your head for days; so I won't say what she said, but she ended with "don't make me come there and take you to the treatments myself". In her mind, me quitting my treatments was not an option and she would make sure it didn't happen. After that conversation, I picked myself up and took my kids to the park! As weird as it sounds, that conversation gave me hope. I knew someone loved me. Someone loved me at one of my lowest points. My friends and family did several things throughout my battle that kept me hopeful when I didn't have the brainpower or energy to do it myself.

I met with a family member concerning my children. I was preparing to write out a bunch of letters that my daughter and son could read throughout their lives. My goal was to write them for certain milestones like dating, birthdays, graduating high school, how to do laundry, wedding days, and when they had children of their own. These letters were to be given to them at these pivotal points in their lives, had I not made it through my battle with breast cancer. We talked about my life insurance policies and how often the family was to visit with them. We also discussed what to give my kids for their milestone birthdays. Have you ever had to contemplate those things? It broke my heart to have to experience it, but it was something that I felt I had to do for them.

When we as believers think of getting healed, we often think of it as being instant. I struggled with the thought that I was not instantly healed and had to go through the process. I was expecting God to perform a miracle by way of the cancer battle ending overnight, when the reality was that I had to go through a process. It was in that process that I got to experience God's miracles!

People often wonder why I don't like the color pink when associated with breast cancer awareness month. That pink ribbon does not represent cancer, in my opinion. That is not the color that I saw when I went for my chemo treatments. The palms of my hands, nail beds and soles of my feet were black. I saw red coming from that dreadful bag, down through the tubes and into my veins ...... RED. I never saw pink-
Mercedes Wilson

MY HURTS

_____

_____

_____

_____

_____

_____

_____

_____

_____

_____

_____

_____

_____

_____

_____

_____

_____

_____

_____

_____

<u>My venting journal entry written on 5-25-2010</u>

What do you say for a broken heart to heal?

How do you convince yourself that everything's ok?

How do you get up every morning and get ready to face the day alone?

Put the pieces of you back together but time on your own?

Find yourself in the maze you call your life.

Have something to offer that's worth value.

It's in the quiet time that I can earn begin
to think and I have to tell myself:

Sadie it's ok to be alone …

There's so much noise all around me.

I'm trying to figure it all out.

I'm driving myself crazy.

Everyone's so loud, why do you have to shout?

It's hard for me to focus but yet I have so much to yet achieve.

I'm asking everyone for advice but have no one to believe.

It's my heart that bleeds and my head that hurts.

Trying to figure it out only makes it worse.

It's my thoughts that are confused

My fears that hold me back.

My loneliness that keeps me running

It's me that has to get me back on track

I need quiet time

Sadie, it's ok to be alone …

I'm going to lay in my own bed tonight, you
know the spot I've been avoiding …

It's ok to be alone.

I'm going to sing songs I like on my way to work.

It's ok to be alone.

I'm going out for ice cream with my kids.

It's ok to be alone.

I'm going to buy myself a ring

It's ok to be alone.

I'm going to get promoted at my job, pray, laugh, go out for margaritas,
hang out with friends, go to new places, and say the whole time:

SADIE it's ok to be alone!

DEEP BREATHE

A journal entry written by me on 10/10/11:

Just started second half of chemo treatments called taxol. I have done bi weekly treatments of Adria + Cytoxin and now 4 doses of taxol then surgery and radiation for 45 days. The first 4 treatments were really rough. First one I lost 3 days worth of memory! Second ok, third and fourth were tough. I felt like I was losing my mind for one week. I have asked God so much throughout this process why? I could have just done surgery but they would have had to remove my whole breast. I asked God to give the doctors wisdom and this is what they recommended. And to think I originally thought these were diabetes symptoms. He set me up! What I thought was a pulled muscle turned out to be CANCER at 28 and I'm being told I've had it for a while. The loneliness and pain is indescribable. How does all this tie into what God has for me? I spoke with deaconess at my church today and she said this is my ministry ... poems, music, songs. I don't know what else to say. I can say, in my pain I have had to resist the urges to go back to ex's! The pains seems unbearable at time and I just want relief, someone to hold me! A physical human being. the pain from the taxol is HORRIBLE! Straight pain from the waist down for 3 days before I got medication that even touched it! And they said this would be the easier chemo! Huh! I have no privacy because I am in so much pain. I can't do anything some days, I hate that! I'm pulling on people and don't want to be a burden. I have great friends and family that helps me keep my mind. Here I am, I'm still standing.

I realized that hope is not birthed from perfection, that hope is started in the depths of your hurting soul with a simple word from God. It is in the hard times that he shows you who he truly is. There is a place in you that no one else can go but God, and in that place, only he can transform and make you new.-Mercedes Wilson

3

HOPE TAKES WORK!

I would love to talk to the person that made our society think that perfection is attainable. Throw out the thought that perfection is what makes you worthy. Perfection requires no work, it just exists. It's you recognizing that you are in need of something greater than yourself, and being willing to work toward it builds hope and success. Work toward becoming a better you and don't be ashamed of your shortcomings, but embrace them and know that you working on you is a part of discovering what you were put here to do. Your ministry of helping others is on the other side of learning you!

For every struggle that I had to endure throughout my life, I had to work harder to overcome it. Please hear me when I say that I could not do any of it without God's intervention. At the same time, he expects us to do our part. Faith is an action word. Sometimes the work is being open to instruction, while other times the work could mean physically doing something to set things into motion on your behalf.

For every situation that I endured, I prayed for, and was given a scripture by God that I rehearsed like it was my job. Some of the scriptures that I leaned on heavily in my toughest times are:

For my divorce and losing my earthly possessions: *"Then the Lord your God will restore your fortunes [in your return from exile], and have*

compassion on you, and will gather you together again from all the peoples (nations) where He has scattered you".
Deuteronomy 30:3;AMP

For my cancer: *"Come to Me, all who are weary and heavily burdened [by religious rituals that provide no peace], and I will give you rest [refreshing your souls with salvation]".* Matthew 11:28;AMP
For my childhood: *"Although my father and my mother have abandoned me, Yet the Lord will take me up [adopt me as His child]".*
Psalm 27:10;AMP

For my anger and mindset toward me and unhealthy relationships after my divorce: *"Be angry [at sin—at immorality, at injustice, at ungodly behavior], yet do not sin; do not let your anger [cause you shame, nor allow it to] last until the sun goes down".*
Ephesians 4:26;AMP

What God thought of me: *"An excellent woman [one who is spiritual, capable, intelligent, and virtuous], who is he who can find her? Her value is more precious than jewels and her worth is far above rubies or pearls. (I event went out and bought myself a ruby ring to wear as a constant reminder!)".*
Proverbs 31:10;AMP

That He was my provider: *"And my God will liberally supply (fill until full) your every need according to His riches in glory in Christ Jesus".*
Philippians 4:19;AMP

That I was hidden and that God was still working on me even at my worst points:" *He made my mouth like a sharpened sword, in the shadow of his hand he hid me; he made me into a polished arrow and concealed me in his quiver".*
Isaiah 49:2;AMP

My work not only came with reading the scriptures, it came with living my life in faith, fully living my life as if these things were going to happen. Have you ever tried to smile when you think you have nothing? When you thought you had your life all figured out, and then just about everything was taken AND now you are battling breast cancer? I didn't want to smile, I wanted to curse people out and stay in my house and cry.

Don't get me wrong, I did slip up and curse people out a couple of times (just being honest). There were days where I prayed much louder than under my breath because my sanity was questionable minute to minute. Some days I had to yell out scriptures to myself and repeated them over and over. I practiced trusting God in all things, thus it became easier (not perfect, but easier).

I spent time alone and learned how good that can be for me. There are times when you feel God has you hidden, and that's exactly the case. When you are at a point of allowing God to make you who He intended you to be, allow Him to be skillful.

Isaiah 49:2;AMP states: *"He made my mouth like a sharpened sword, in the shadow of his hand he hid me; he made me into a polished arrow and concealed me in his quiver"*.

In order for your mindset to change, you can't always be in the company of so many other people. Along with crowds come opinions that stunt your growth. Become comfortable with being alone in certain seasons.

I began to pick up reading during this phase of my trials (I have a list of the books that I read at the end of this book if you would like to read them yourself). I began to view God in a different way! I began to see that the things that I experienced were actually beginning to shape me, that God trusted me to be a light for so many through my obedience to Him. BUT, it started with me first though.

I put effort into being a better me, but doing it God's way. I won't lie, I was on a mission to prove God wrong at one point. I was intentionally obedient to be able to say "aha, see God, you didn't come through like you said!" While I was on a mission to prove God wrong, He showed me myself. He showed me my heart, my pain, my stubbornness, and my rebellion. He also showed me my value in Him, the times in my life where He was there and I didn't recognize it, the things that were in my family line that would end with me, my children's future, and glimpse of mine. He stripped me of myself, my plans, the plans that others had for me, and started the process of rebuilding me!

I realized that hope is not birthed from perfection, that hope is started in the depths of your hurting soul with a simple word from God. It is in the hard times that He shows you who He truly is. There is a place in you that no one else can go but God, and in that place, only He can transform and make you new.

I had an issue with being alone. I also had an issue with anger. I sinned in my anger on a regular basis. That anger is what drove me to have relationships that weren't healthy. I allowed myself to date men that had no interest in anything long term, but the kicker was, at times, the feeling was mutual! My goal was to get what I felt that I deserved, which was attention, love, companionship, and sex. After all, I deserved to be happy, right? My work came from allowing God to hide me and deal with me one-on-one. It was when I acknowledged my disappointment to God about Him that He began to show me Mercedes.

I had to shut down the dating for a while. I stayed home more, and in the downtime, learned more about me and what I liked. As a woman, I naturally wanted to be made whole by a companion, and that sounded good to me at the time. At that point in my life, I didn't realize the dysfunction in that statement. No one person made me whole! I needed to be a complete young woman BEFORE the right man came into my life. I didn't trust myself or my decisions when it came to men. I recognized that I clearly needed some help from God, so I made a choice to be alone.

There were certain things that I wanted to learn about myself before I entered into the next relationship: what my favorite color was (I am still trying to figure that out), my favorite music, the types of books I liked to read, how often I wanted to pamper myself, what types of friends I wanted, what do my kids enjoyed doing together, whether or not I had the guts to go to the movies alone, or if I was even comfortable eating at a restaurant by myself. I was on a mission to learn myself and cried for a while when doing these things ALONE.

Soul ties

I had to deal with all of the soul ties that I had brought into my life. Sex is one way of forming these, but I also experienced these in my mind.

When I decided to have a time of no dating, some feelings that I had needed to be dealt with. I had involved myself in relationships that I knew from the beginning were not correct. During one particular fast I was taking part in, I was reminded of some of the ungodly conversations I'd had, and how I allowed these things to infiltrate my mind and my heart. (These had to be dealt with before any man that would want to call me his wife could enter the picture.)How unfair it is for any man to enter a relationship where other men have occupancy? When a woman moves from one relationship right on to another one, without first working on herself from the previous one, she WILL carry things with her.

This was a tough lesson for me, and I repented for not only allowing this to be a part of my life for so long, but for also disrespecting my body. Respecting the process of addressing my soul ties came with a freedom that released me from other areas as well … like my anger! Freedom feels so good!

Forgiving others

The next issue was my unforgiveness! As much as I thought that I had moved on with my life from my childhood, I was carrying a big bag of self-pity and hatred. This was also another component of why I was so angry. I could not understand how someone's innocence could be taken and everyone else just goes on with life. I had a "someone has to pay for this" attitude. I often wanted vengeance, and those thoughts weren't nice. God was not moving quick enough for me. I had always heard the quote "forgiveness is for you, not the other person" and that phrase, in my opinion, was for the weak.

God had to show me myself. Not only does unforgiveness cloud your judgement, but it also allows you to wallow in self-pity. I felt as though others' decisions that were out of my control had ruined my life, and now my life was thrown back into my lap for ME to deal with. I was holding a mess of a life and had to clear my mind and heart of these feelings that came along with it. I considered myself a victim. When it is all said and done, Christ's blood covered us all, who was I to determine what was covered and what wasn't? Christ's blood came with no conditions. That was a very hard pill to swallow when you are hurting, but it's still the truth.

A piece of my true freedom came with forgiving those that had hurt me, whether I received an apology or not. I used to write letters to get out my frustrations and then rip them up so no one would ever see them. In 2015, I wrote letters to those that I forgave, listed the things that I forgave them for line by line, and mailed them! I needed to forgive and have it on record for myself. The biggest challenge for me was forgiving the person that sexually molested me. I had to come to the realization that my unforgiveness was holding ME back, not the person. Releasing that person from what they had done to me and what was taken from me gave me my strength back. What others do to hurt you is not on you!

I refused to allow my past to be replayed in my mind, instead I took that and allowed God to turn it around and use it for His glory. It no longer mattered if I ever got an apology. I prayed for this person's soul at that point, and moved on.

The estranged relationships that I had with loved ones changed. I opened my heart to loving family once again. The fact of the matter is that I wanted a relationship with my father, but due to my lack of trust, I was guarded. I felt abandoned, left alone at one of the hardest points of my life, and unprotected as a child. While all of those things may have been true, the fact of the matter was that sometimes others are hurting as well. My parents had me at a very young age, they were babies themselves.

My father and I got to talk about where we both were at that point in our lives. We both acknowledged the hurt and pain that we felt, and decided to give our relationship another chance. The weird thing was, at that point in my life, while I appreciated it, I no longer needed an apology. Our talking allowed my heart to be further softened and I fully let go.

I had to let go of setting unrealistic expectations on people and let God be God. It's a lot harder than it sounds but it's so true. Once I allowed myself to feel the grief that I had held in for so long I was able to heal and not judge. You can't be healed in something that you don't first show forgiveness toward.

Forgive yourself

Forgive yourself, please forgive yourself. One thing that is sometimes harder than forgiving others is forgiving yourself! We have all had those "what was I thinking" moments. We are always our own worst critic, and in areas that we have grace for others we tend to be harder on ourselves. Until recently, I had not forgiven myself on my choices of relationships. I can now admit that I picked the wrong people to allow in my personal space, and let them occupy that space way longer than what I should have. I was taken for granted, my love abused, cheated on, and also made to feel like everything about me was wrong. I was looking for approval, and always seeking something from others that I should have done for myself by learning who I was in Christ! I talked friends' ears off about the mistreatment so much that I know it drove them nuts. I was embarrassed in front of family in ways that no woman should ever be, and used only for what I could offer financially. My job was constantly finding the next thing that I could do to be accepted, appreciated, and loved. When I got tired of that, then I came to my senses and said "No more". The problem with that is I gave up years of my life. Most people stay in abusive relationships because they feel as though they have invested so much time with this one person and no one else will want them. NOT TRUE! I was guilty of thinking all of this and stayed in relationships way longer than I should have.

If it were someone else that told me all of this I would say "don't feel bad, that's where you were at that point in your life, be glad that you finally woke up and moved on". We all tend to date or marry the people that we do based on where we are in our lives. If you have low self-esteem, most likely your relationship choices reflect that. Letting people abuse your time, love, and money reflects how you feel about yourself. Acknowledge that and forgive yourself now that you know better! There are always two sides to every story, so take accountability of what you could have done better, then you forgive yourself to make sure you get the lesson that is supposed to come from it. Sometimes the lesson is setting up boundaries to avoid toxic relationships.

There was a certain person, whose texts would always ruin my day. They were upset at my new zeal for not allowing anyone to abuse me any longer. When I tell you, I allowed this person to put me through hell, that is no exaggeration. I felt threatened in multiple ways. That was a very eye-opening experience, because when I got tired of feeling that way, I realized my peace was one thing that was being robbed. I realized that I no longer wanted to allow that behavior to bother me; however, there was something preventing me from doing that, and then it hit me … I needed to get over being angry at myself. Once I acknowledged that, forgiving myself came a little easier. When that forgiveness came it was like a light bulb came on.

I have come to realize that while not perfect, I am a marvelous mother, great wife, a thoughtful friend, a good cook, a caring community servant leader, and I am a very hard worker. But guess what? I know that without anyone having to tell me or confirm that, and that is the difference! I forgave myself for making bad decisions on who I gave my heart to. I recognized where I was at that point of my life, and I thanked God that He removed the scales off of my eyes to show me who I really was in Him. The same grace that you give to others you need to extend to yourself.

When you forgive yourself, the actions of those in your past no longer bother you. Your headspace is totally different, and you no longer want to take part in something that does not build you up the way that God wants you to be. You will have a lot more peace.

Whenever God allowed me to go through things, He gave me a glimpse of my future, of what could be if I allowed Him to be a part of this decision. It has never been easy, but I can guarantee you that anything that is done in obedience to Him will be lasting.

I also had what my husband likes to call "Super woman" mentality. She still peeks her head up every now and then. It was my children and I for about 4 years, and I had to do everything when they were with me.

Friends helped where they could, but for the most part, if I didn't do it then it wouldn't get done. Anyone that dates a single parent is in for a unique challenge. I was determined to not bring any man around my children until I counted him worthy, so I was extra hard on them. I made it clear that I did not need them, and that if things weren't going to be my way they could keep it moving! The problem with that, it's not what I really wanted. I wanted someone to rescue me from my hurt AND get through the wall that I put up! No one was ever going to make it with me long term, even though love is what I really wanted.

The work with the "super woman" mentality was long and tough. God had to show me my imperfections and then tell me that the man that he had for me was imperfect as well. I was not the only person in the equation and grace was in order. No man wants to be in a relationship where he is not needed, and just like I wanted respect, so would the man that I would want to be with. I needed to be reminded of that. God bless the person that has to deal with a single parent. We make you work!

Forgiveness does not mean agreement. You can be against an act that someone committed toward you while not allowing their actions to impact your next move. Unforgiveness caused me to hold grudges which in turn caused me to sin due to my victim mentality. I had to make a habit to forgive myself and others like God forgives us all. My mind is clearer and my heart is so much more open when I forgive others. I am always ready for what God has next for me because of that!-Mercedes Wilson

WHAT I NEED TO WORK ON

<u>Journal entry written by me on 7/12/2010</u>

I tell you what … dealing with insecurities is a (explicative). The definition is: not firm on or fairly fixed; likely to fail or give way. What should I do about this relationship? I need friends! Work is challenging but I like it, I need to take care of my money. I am afraid of the pain I am going to feel when I have to face the alone time! The relationship that I am in right now moved so fast, and I think that I used him to fill void so that I didn't have to deal with the pain. I met my children's father when I was 16 years old and I am now 27 years old with 2 children, a failed marriage and no money. So I have to start with what I do have! I have my children that love me! I have a career that I have worked hard for … I have to build off of that. I just don't know what to do about this relationship! I have been dealt a whole new hand of cards and have to figure out how to play them! By myself! I have to start by loving myself, respecting myself, finding myself!

4

USE YOUR AMMUNITION. GUARD YOUR PEACE.

I love the quote by Kobe Bryant, "Everything negative - pressure, challenges - is all an opportunity for me to rise."

Anyone that aspires to do anything great understands that the success is in the details. Nothing great happens overnight, and I truly believe that every situation that you encounter is to prepare you for what you are becoming.

I have a strong dislike for quick fix messages. I also have a strong dislike for speeches or books that encourage doing better but don't provide directions on how to achieve it. I learned how to find the great things that were inside of me in stages.

The first stage for me was learning I am human. Perfection is not in our DNA.

I worked for a corporation for 7 years before I left and went full time to focus on my non-profit organization. I had to leave, because after my battle with breast cancer I could no longer keep up in such a fast- paced workplace. I had also lost a lot of memory due to the chemotherapy treatments (chemo brain is real folks).

I planned on retiring from my corporate job, so leaving was a very tough move for me. I cried for a very long time because I missed the sales environment, my staff, the trainings and staff development, relationships with my peers, team building activities, and the rush that I got when we hit goals. I missed the capabilities my mind before cancer, and losing the ability to move and think like I used to was a life altering change.

While still working at my corporate job, I started a non-profit organization called For Our Daughters Inc. I decided to use my cancer diagnosis to help others. Leaving this job also gave me the freedom to focus on growing the non-profit organization. I had learned a lot about how to talk to others, show them the benefits of supporting us, how to create a teamwork atmosphere, and how to work very hard. The mission of For Our Daughters Inc is to educate young women on how to advocate about their own health and wellness.....something that I had no idea how to do before my diagnosis. I worked a lot of late nights on For Our Daughters Inc. and didn't think twice about it. I used what I knew to turn my situation around and turned a negative situation into ammunition to help others. When For Our Daughters Inc(FOD) started in 2012, we reached 700 students and in 2017 FOD reached over 1,650 young women with our message of educating young women on how to advocate for their health and wellness thanks to my previous job experience!

Guard what you have worked for. When you are hoping for something and start working for it, it only makes sense to protect your progress. Preserve what you have experienced so you can testify about your story of survival whenever the opportunity presents itself. The bible says: ... *"for his mouth speaks from the overflow of his heart"*. Luke 6:45;AMP.

Sometimes more heart work had to be done, so I had to be quiet until God worked certain things out on the inside of me. Hope can be the feeling you get in your gut when wanting the best in a situation. We can at times talk ourselves right out of our own blessing.

Matthew 17:20;AMP says: *"Because of your little faith [your lack of trust and confidence in the power of God]; for I assure you and most solemnly say to you, if you have [living] faith the size of a mustard seed, you will say to this mountain, 'Move from here to there,' and [if it is God's will] it will move; and nothing will be impossible for you"*. So, imagine the damage we can do with speaking against our own progress. Protect your testimony!

Protecting your peace is equally as important. Peace doesn't equal silence and lack of hard work; it represents a calmness in your heart. Your heart harbors your life. Proverbs 13:3 AMP says, *"The one who guards his mouth [thinking before he speaks] protects his life; The one who opens his lips wide [and chatters without thinking] comes to ruin".*

Use wisdom in your conversations, the company that you keep, and what YOU allow you to say about you! Fight for your peace.

Maintaining your peace has to be worked on. When you fully submit your life to God, things will shift, people will be removed, and your lifestyle will most likely be redirected. God not only shows you how to secure your peace, but also, how to keep it. There were friendships that I thought would last a lifetime; however, they ended up being seasonal. There is a stability that comes with allowing God to direct your relationships. I have grown to love it! There is no place that I know to be safer than within the will of God.

Always being on the defense gets tiring. That means you always wait for the next attack or tragedy to happen. I prefer to be on the offense. Learning the patterns of God teaches you that He always prepares you for what's about to come. Not saying there won't be surprises, but we are always equipped to deal with them. How does God get the glory if I am always drowning him with my sorrows? If I am always seeking what He told me is mine, then anything that gets in my way better prepares me to properly use what's coming. Learn how to use what you are given to prevent abuse-Mercedes Wilson

My ammunition

5

CHANGING YOUR MINDSET CHANGES YOUR VIEW

The way that we see things begins in the womb. The visual system is the most complex sensory system in the human body, however is the least mature at birth. We have to learn how to use our eyes and we learn by patterns and applying meaning to objects(healthofchildren.com).

We get to physically see things AFTER they manifest in the atmosphere around us. What we know to be faith teaches the opposite of that. We are challenged by God to see things in the Spirit and call things forth BEFORE they come to pass. I dare you to set the patterns in your mind and heart from the word received from God about your life and watch your atmosphere change! We are conditioned to want to see things beforehand, and as a result, miss out on so many miracles.

Do you think positive in a situation that doesn't look good? One of the hardest scriptures for me to live is Philippians 4:8. It reads: *"Finally, believers, whatever is true, whatever is honorable and worthy of respect, whatever is right and confirmed by God's word, whatever is pure and wholesome, whatever is lovely and brings peace, whatever is admirable and of good repute; if there is any excellence, if there is anything worthy of praise, think continually on these things [center your mind on them, and implant them in your heart]".*

We have all heard about how the renewing of the mind must take place in believers. You don't even have to be a believer in any certain religion for the fruit of your mindset to manifest in your life. Your mind controls how you see things, and it is through that lens that you can change the course of your life.

There were many days that I literally had nothing to think about because there was nothing good. I purposely tried not to think, but I could only do that for so long. I eventually got to the point where I wanted to live and be happy, so my days changed from purposely trying not to think into purposely trying to think of one good thing. I would think on that one good thing for a full day. I would allow myself to feel the joy that came with it. I would share my excitement about it, no matter how small, with a friend. I would get up the next day and find another thing to think on that was lovely and keep that with me all day as well. Before I knew it, I was starting to make plans for my life and looked forward to finding positive things to think on! One of the times that was very hard for me was being single after God dealt with my anger from my divorce. I was angry every single Friday evening that I did not have my children. My words to God every single Friday were "wow, I am such a great woman that I have to spend my Friday's alone huh?"

After so long of not thinking good thoughts, I started planning my Fridays. I was intentional with my thinking. I started out by thinking about what I wanted for dinner that night. I would think about what kind of meal I wanted to make for myself, the wine that I wanted to drink with it, the movie that I wanted to watch, if I wanted to do a candlelit bubble bath beforehand, and what time I wanted to sleep in until the next day. These things were lovely, to me so I thought about them instead of what I usually did on my Fridays alone.

After a couple of Fridays doing this I realized I was looking forward to these movie nights. I would get excited about getting a RedBox movie after work, (which I always ended up paying twenty-five dollars for because I never returned them), curling up under a blanket and watching a good Tyler Perry movie! I still had my moments where I wanted companionship, don't get me wrong, but I made an effort to learn to be content and happy by myself. My view was starting to change when I changed my mindset.

2 corinthians 10:5 says: *"Casting down imaginations, and every high thing that exalteth itself against the knowledge of God, and bringing into captivity every thought to the obedience of Christ…"*. I was experiencing victory!

I often repented for trying so hard to be someone else, when God took so much time at crafting me. When there is a broken appliance in your home you go the manufacturer to repair it, no one else! So why, for so long, have I gone to others to fix what only God can?-Mercedes Wilson

6

HOPE PREPARES YOU FOR THE NEW

I love the story in Matthew 25 about the man that was traveling into a far country and called his servants to give them talents to look over while he was away.

He gave one servant 5 talents, another two, and the last he gave one. The bible says he gave to each man according to his TALENTS.

**Sidebar: When you go through challenges, God always brings out things on the inside of you that you didn't know were there, and then expects you to use them.

The servant that received five talents did some work and doubled what he had. The one that received two did the same. The servant that received one talent made a hole in the ground and hid it. He did nothing with what he was given, he produced no growth.

When the master returned he came for what was his plus some! To the two that doubled what they were given, they were made rulers over many things and entered into the joy of the Lord.

The last servant that hid his talents proclaimed that he was afraid of the leader because he knew that he was harsh in dealings with others. He brought him his one talent that he was given and seemed content with that! He was called slothful and reprimanded. The one talent that he had was taken and given to the servant that doubled his to 10. The new things that you desire are on the other side of managing what you have right in front of you!

Your gift is constantly working on your behalf, setting up new opportunities and waiting for you to come and get it! The bible clearly states that "A man's gift [given in love or courtesy] makes room for him And brings him before great men", Proverbs 18:16;AMP

At one of my previous jobs our VP used to do pop up store visits on a regular basis. He wasn't your average VP because he genuinely cared. When I came back from my leave with breast cancer and told everyone about wanting to start For Our Daughters Inc, he made sure I had everything I needed to get the org started He appointed people that worked for him to help me get what I needed.

During these pop up visits, would check things that average leaders didn't. I got the rundown of what he looked for and stayed prepared should he show up. He believed in checking things that managers don't think to have clean when the big wigs came through, like the microwave. So, guess what I did? I made sure my microwave along with all other things were always ready for a visit. I was not going to miss my chance at a new door.

Always be ready to use what you have, because God will come back to see what you have done with what he has given you.

When For Our Daughters Inc. was first started we looked for media opportunities. We got the attention of several local TV stations and started going on a game show that really highlighted great organizations in the community. It was there that my ability to be a television personality was discovered. We nourished the relationship with the television station with no intention of doing anything more than what we agreed upon, but God saw my work! I was approached about being a cohost for a daily talk show ... WHAT??? My gift made room for me!

I like being uncomfortable now! For years I wondered if my tendency to get bored easily during a task was a flaw … nope, that's God's way of making sure that I stay moving. When I become complacent, that means I am not tuning into what He is saying anymore. My end goal is to please God, and if there is no work attached to it, it's not faith.-Mercedes Wilson

OPPORTUNITIES OF INCREASE THAT I CAN ACT ON

7

EMPATHY AND RESTORATION ALWAYS FOLLOW TRIALS

One of the things that I love about God is his ability to teach you empathy from your experiences. When I was going through cancer, I learned so much about suffering that my whole perception of others changed. To have the ability to see things from a perspective other than your own is a major asset. Cancer taught me empathy toward those that suffer. Certain pains are necessary for us to experience God's process for our lives, and during that process we are changed to our core. Cancer taught me about struggle. Cancer also taught me that I was not defective. For so long I thought that others were looking at me like I was a bad woman because I had to go through the process of cancer even though I was a Christian. Shouldn't we be instantly healed? How can I endure sickness but love God? For all of you out there that may be experiencing condemnation for being human and going through something, I understand you and want to say that you are not defective. I learned through my process of cancer that my view of God changed along with my outlook on life. They changed in a way that has made me a better woman. Restoration surfaced when I came to terms with the fact that the bigger the trial, the more God can trust you with what is coming on the other side of it! It also releases you from judging others. How many of us have been judged by someone that has never gone through our mess? Their judgement hurt, right? No matter what you say to try to help them understand, they will never get it. With empathy comes the ability to forgive, and that includes forgiving yourself!

In my process of forgiving myself, my eyes were opened to pain, and how others react to pain. The time I went back into my old home that I had lost was a forgiving myself moment. I acknowledged the things that brought me to that point, and had a great cry that released me to feel the pain and disappointment. That cry opened me up to a place of vulnerability that only God could make right. It also did something else, it changed my perception of anyone that had lost anything they worked very hard for. Being vulnerable truly feels like open heart surgery, it's a feeling that you can't easily forget. If that isn't enough to cause you to show empathy, then I don't know what is!

We have all been and will continue to be in a place where we need forgiveness. The bible says: *"If we say that we have no sin, we deceive ourselves, and the truth is not in us"* (John 1:8;KJV).

Empathy allows you to see the imperfections in others and have the ability to admit that you were once there.

For years I was angry at the women in my life. I used to question how they could not know better, or do better? I would question their choices of relationships and how they couldn't see their worth. That is, until I experienced my divorce. I was driving to another city to visit a man that was not someone that I was supposed to be around at all. I had a moment where I asked myself "Mercedes what are you doing?" I knew that this was going nowhere and that I wanted to do better. I stopped at that moment to acknowledge where I was in my life and how vulnerable I was…that was the moment that God said to me "The vulnerability you are experiencing is what other women feel". I was fully aware of how I was trying to fill a void in my life and heart, and that I was attempting to use a man do it. I should have turned around and went back home at that moment but I still took that trip. The whole way there and back I regretted it. I still remember the hole I felt in my heart during the drive. My heart was instantly softened, and so was my judgment toward the women that I questioned in my life.

Allow God to show you yourself and you will be surprised at how he can free you from so many other things in your life.

HOPE

There's no way you can fully move forward with being healed on the inside without changing your view of others. It's very easy for vulnerable women to allow men into their hearts and bodies that don't deserve to be there. I will never look at another woman in disappointment about staying in a dysfunctional relationship. I look at her with empathy and hope for restoration in her life. You can truly reach people when they know that you care and that you can relate.

I know what it feels like to be in need. "Not enough" was my friend for a long time. I know the fear of not being able to feed my children if I didn't perform well enough. I know the humble spirit that it takes to have to accept help on a regular basis from those around you because you are not capable of taking care of yourself. I smile when I share, give others the same quality of respect and care that I would want to receive, try my best to encourage those that look like their hope is a little low, and empathize with those in the toughest parts of their faith walk. After all, it's a part of the reason that the hardest times in my life couldn't take me out ... God's not done with me yet-Mercedes Wilson

8

ALWAYS GIVE BACK

"He that hath pity upon the poor lendeth unto the LORD; and that which he hath given will he pay him again"(proverbs 19:17;KJV).

It is not a secret that the laws of reciprocity are still in effect. In my years of service, one thing that always rings true is people's desire to be a part of something bigger than themselves. Very few people dislike how they feel after helping someone in need. Helping those in need is something that God smiles upon.

Since I was a young girl I have wanted to help other young women. I had the ability to recognize when someone was hurting. I never cared about their skin color, or socioeconomic status, hurt was hurt.

College was when I knew for sure that one day I would help other young women. In my college days, I would ride by vacant houses and catch myself pulled over looking at it, and envisioning it being a home for young women. I was drawn to the "why". Knowing that someone was hurting wasn't enough, I wanted to know what caused it and how I could help. Hope is able to be felt, seen, and acted on.

I had no clue how this would come to pass, but I researched organizations that did what I desired to do. When I joined a local church, I studied the women's group leader and how she formed relationships with the other women. I picked her brain and watched her operate in her gifts of loving others. She gave back, she was there when we needed her, and she sacrificed her time and heart to see that we were at peace in our lives. She challenged us to become better even when it was difficult. She also celebrated with us in our victories, she gave back! It helped us grow into the women that we were on our way to being, women that helped others.

When you give back to others you are sowing seeds for them to help someone else. When you build up someone else, again, you are sowing seeds to help them reciprocate it in someone else's life.

We recently had a guest at my church that came to speak about her organization. While speaking she called me out and said that she remembered when she first had the idea to start a non-profit and someone told her to reach out to me. She recalled when she reached out to me and I invited her out to a local coffee house. We sat and talked and I gave her a lot of information on how to get a organization up and going. It hit me hard when she recounted this, because I never thought it helped her the way that it did. That was a moment where God said "see, you sowed seeds". I was fighting hard to hold back the tears, because I knew that by doing that I pleased God.

Proverbs 3:27;KJV states: "Withhold not good from them to whom it is due, when it is in the power of thine hand to do it". When hope is acted on and you see the fruit of it in your life, don't withhold it.

I have been accused all of my life of giving too much of myself to my own detriment. I consider that to be true. I would give out of my lack of emotional stability, out of my hurt, out of my longing to have love myself. Because those that did not have good intentions recognized that, my love was misused. When I took the time away to get Mercedes correct, then I could love from a pure place and could form boundaries. You can't give something that you don't have, so I learned the hard way how to give from a healed place.

Doing good for someone is not always about money. A lot of times it's your resources by way of time or talents. There have been times where I know someone is hurting, and I take out to time to call them and just see how they are doing. Maybe giving back is cooking a meal for someone that you know is struggling with the loss of a loved one. Your gifts and accolades mean nothing if you don't have love and the ability to use what you have to help others from a pure place.

1 Corinthians 13:1-7;KJV

"Though I speak with the tongues of men and of angels, and have not charity, I am become as sounding brass, or a tinkling cymbal.

And though I have the gift of prophecy, and understand all mysteries, and all knowledge; and though I have all faith, so that I could remove mountains, and have not charity, I am nothing.

And though I bestow all my goods to feed the poor, and though I give my body to be burned, and have not charity, it profiteth me nothing.

Charity suffereth long, and is kind; charity envieth not; charity vaunteth not itself, is not puffed up,

Doth not behave itself unseemly, seeketh not her own, is not easily provoked, thinketh no evil;

Rejoiceth not in iniquity, but rejoiceth in the truth;

Beareth all things, believeth all things, hopeth all things, endureth all things".

Make sure that you are healed before giving back by way of advice. We all want to share the results of a tough situation with the desire to help others, but please be careful of your heart before you do so. If there is one thing that I don't like, it's when people give you advice from a hurt or angry place. I don't consider that sound advice, I consider those venting sessions. In James 3:17;KJV it states: *"But the wisdom from above is first pure, then peaceable, gentle, open to reason, full of mercy and good fruits, impartial and sincere".* Please look at what sound advice includes! Even if it is a situation where someone needs to take drastic measures in their life, the spirit in which the instruction is coming from should be nothing less than what is listed above in James. When giving advice to someone you have the power to change the course of their lives by your words. So, if you are not in a good place pertaining to giving advice, be honest and say that. Sometimes the best answer is "you really don't want my advice on this because I am not in a good place". I have heard that a lot and respected the person for being honest.

On the other hand, sound advice can do several things. It can calm a person down who may be worked up because they realize that it is going to be ok. Sound advice can also help a person realize that they are not alone. Being able to relate to someone and showing yourself as an example helps. Finally, sound advice can propel someone toward success. When someone can see that you overcame a situation and came out better, it plants the seed of success in them. When they see you, they will see the fruits of success; and you all know we love to see good fruit in the life of someone that is giving us advice.

I can't tell you how many nights I cried myself to sleep because of my circumstances. I also can't tell you how many nights that because of my transparency with God, that he met me where I was and comforted me. It was those "hugs" in the midnight hours that helped me make it through. I woke up with songs on my mind that were from God, they were a reminder of his heart toward me. Those were the best songs that I have ever heard!-Mercedes Wilson

9

GUESS WHAT? YOU WILL NEED HELP!

Proverbs 11:14;KJV says: *"Where no counsel is, the people fall: but in the multitude of counsellors there is safety"*. I grew up hearing that counseling was not needed; you don't need to tell anyone your personal business. That could not be any further from the truth. Also, physicians weren't trusted, so therefore, the only time someone went to see one was when it was a life or death situation. It was only when things became unbearable in life for me that I took a chance at going to a doctor and get help. As a young woman, there were people in my community that I was referred to by word of mouth to give me counseling, and it truly helped me avoid a nervous breakdown. They met with me periodically to, at first, give me coping mechanisms and best practices for different stages of my life. There were times where the counselor and I would meet alone and he/she would tell me things that made me focus on certain parts of my life. Those meetings normally upset me, especially when I felt as though I was not in the wrong. As I took the time and started to put advice to practice in my life, I started to see change within myself. There was peace that came with having counsel from the right person.

I also grew up in a time where you didn't reveal your issues because it was considered sign of weakness. I was not used to talking about health, relationships, sex, how to deal with anger, etc. Because of my lack of communication skills, I feel as though I didn't mature, and I was stunted in areas where communication was crucial in being productive in life. I was ashamed of getting counsel at first, but one thing that made me continue was the fact that I was hurting so bad and needed someone to help me sort through all of these feelings.

The counselor quickly identified that there were some unresolved issues in my past. I was able to sort through a lot of the why's in my life and heal. I learned that there was safety in talking to someone that has not only studied the human brain, but knows how to help you sort through some of the toughest most confusing times of your life. I left so many sessions feeling vulnerable. At times I needed to hear myself say things out loud to realize how foolish some of my thoughts were. As I disclosed the events of my life, I started to see common themes, and that revelation allowed me to see what changes had to be made.

My husband and I still go to marriage counseling even though we have been married for over 3 years. Our belief is if we stay proactive about our relationship, we will get to discover things about each other that will help our marriage stay strong. There's no one that can tell me that the proper counseling is something to be embarrassed or ashamed about. The same way that I seek help with my organization if I have questions or need to learn something, is the same way that I approach my marriage. My family is worth it!

God has appointed people in all walks of life to assist us, and we shortchange ourselves with our man-made limitations. I learned how to trust myself and my decisions; I learned my triggers, my shortcomings, my strengths, and how to effectively identify those that needed to be in my life.

I can't even imagine if I had the mindset of not needing help when it came to my cancer diagnosis. My children would be without a mother right now. I prayed for my doctors to have wisdom and followed their instruction with the belief that they were there to keep me around for my purpose. I am able to do what I do with my children thanks to the doctors' expertise and ability to follow their hearts to do what they were put here to do. There were only a couple of times that I said no to my doctors, and that was when they wanted to give me medicine to calm me down before my chemo treatments. I couldn't make it 100% easy for them, so I chose the small stuff. There was a scan I got a few years after my cancer diagnosis that showed a spot they thought was a reoccurrence. I went to the appointments after that scan and the doctors told me that I had to have surgery to remove this. I did not want to go, I cried, prayed, cried, and prayed again, but I also listened to what my doctors said. The day that I went for my surgery, they prepped me and got me set up. They had to scan again to be able to mark the area in my breast that needed to be operated on that morning. The spot was gone!!!! I learned such a great lesson that day! The doctors were amazed and said they had never experienced that. They were sure that someone was working on my behalf. I listened to their counsel, against my will, because I trusted and prayed for them on a regular basis; and God showed up in that situation!

Sometimes that counsel will come by way of a good friend, a sounding board. There are certain people that are set up in my life to keep me grounded. The ones that are very wise and patient, they love God, and I can see the fruits of the spirit in their lives. We need them, I need them! My emotions will fool me a lot of the time because I am caught up in the moment. Sometimes a different perspective can give you a big picture look and bring you back to reality. One thing that I know to be true is that your emotions will lie to you. Not only will they lie to you, but they will change on you, and proper counsel can set you straight.

Proverbs 25:8;KJV He that [hath] no rule over his own spirit [is like] a city [that is] broken down, [and] without walls.

WE NEED COUNSEL!!!

I always pray for the wisdom to determine who should be pouring into my life. Does you life represent the God that we serve? I do my best not to judge, but when it comes to someone pouring into me, I am a fruit inspector for sure!- Mercedes Wilson

10

IT'S NOT OVER YET!

Many of us learn, at some point in our lives, what we were put here to do. By changing your perspective on your hardships, you will quickly realize that once you have an idea of your purpose the trials that quickly follow are just part of your making. Allow your trials to make you a better person and propel you into your destiny. Makeovers only happen when you are "made over". Pressure brings out the things in you that need to be dealt with before the next stages of your life. You would only abuse what is to come if you don't learn how to treat it accordingly.

When I was in elementary school my teacher asked the whole class to print out what we wanted to do when we grew up. They had these digital cut outs that we could paste under our heads to signify what type of career that we wanted to have. Some pasted fireman suits and police officer uniforms. I created a magazine cover and put a woman's body with a skirt suit under my head. I knew that I wanted to be on the cover of a magazine for something business related. I carried that picture with me until I was an adult. I carried it through all of the tough times in my life as a reminder to myself that one day my dream will come true!

If not for the experiences in my childhood I would not have been empathetic enough to help young women today. The mission of the organization that I am the Founder and Executive Director of, For Our Daughters Inc. is educating young women on how to advocate for their own health and wellness. Being able to relate to a young woman in pain is what makes the difference in what I do. To have the privilege to lend a ear to a young women is priceless. I get to be, for so many young women, what I needed growing up.

Hearing their stories pulls at the strings of my heart. There is one story of a mother daughter success from our program that always makes me tear up. This mother and daughter had not had much of a productive conversation in years, and the daughter was closed up and unwilling to do anything any different to improve their relationship. After one of our workshops this young woman went home and sat with her mother to converse. The mother emailed me the next day and expressed to me how she was crying as she was typing the email because "she got her baby back." These are the stories that we often hear from parents that make me realize my pain was not in vain.

There is an organization in Buffalo that I recently visited. I spoke to young women that were truly hurting and in the foster care system. They looked at me with a look of "what is this lady going to teach us, she doesn't know my pain". When I shared my story, their demeanors changed immediately, and they opened up and were able to share. It's the times like those that make what I had to go through worth it. It's those times where you can see the look of hope on the face of a young woman that makes my heart melt. All hope is not lost, so don't count yourself out.

If I had never gone through breast cancer, then I would have never started For Our Daughters Inc. If not for a story of survival, there would never have been any magazine covers, thus giving the organization the exposure that it needed for growth. If FOD was not in existence then I would not have started my career in television. From my television career, I had the opportunity to put together my first magazine issue. Without the experience from the magazine issue, this book would not be in existence!

Without ever experiencing divorce, I wouldn't have learned what I know about myself. I wouldn't have the amazing husband that I have right now, or expanded my family again. I was told that I may never have babies again after the chemotherapy, but we had twin girls! These girls taught us about God's grace. Not only have I felt the pain of two miscarriages, but I have felt the joy of my body over performing and having twins. From the pain that I experienced by losing two babies, God gave them right back to me! It's not over!

Experiencing a divorce brought me to a place of being humble that I had never experienced before. I am now able to experience love in a new way with someone that is in the game just as much as I am. The love, patience and compassion that my husband shows is unmatched by any love (outside of God's love) that I have ever had.

I remember our first date. My husband almost ran me off with his confidence that I was going to be his wife. He pursued me, courted me, made it very clear that I did not have to convince him of my work because he saw it all by himself. It's not over!

Had it not been for my bankruptcy, I wouldn't know what it is like to lose everything that you have. There's times in your life where you are broken just to be built back up again. To be able to recognize and empathize with someone that is going through a rough patch can mean life or death to them. Desperation can make a seemingly happy person do things that you could never imagine. Being able to relate and show someone that when you are at your worst, the only place that you can go is up, gives them the strength needed to keep going. I have learned to see that the old cliche "the darkest hour comes before the break of day" is very true. I now know that when things seem unbearable, if I hold on a little longer, I will get to see the goodness that is due. Sometimes some of these encouraging sayings in their dark hours are needed ... I can relate, I feel your pain, and you will live to see the good things that God has in store for you!

My life is a story of failures, hurt, pain, hard work, faith, triumph, and overcoming obstacles. I can tell you one thing for sure, that my perception of trying situations and circumstances has changed. Whatever challenges me is a part of what is going to propel me.

YOU can do this! You just need a lot of work and just a little bit of HOPE!

No one can tell me that God is not a miracle worker. I have seen him in action with my own eyes-Mercedes Wilson

11

MY NEW

After the period of choosing to not date I was in the kitchen with my son, and out of nowhere he asks "Mom, when are you going to start dating?" At first, I was shocked, because what 10 year old asks that question? Mine! My children saw me working very hard at raising them and when they were ready they realized that it was important to them to see me happy too. I seized that moment to have this conversation with my son and daughter. I asked Isaiah where that question came from and he said, "we never see you with anyone". Fighting back tears I told them both that it was important to me to not bring anyone in their lives until I knew that man was worthy to be in their presence. I asked him what he would want to see in any man that I brought to meet them. Isaiah thought about it for a few seconds and said, " he has to like basketball, treat you and Gabby good, like spending time and playing with us". I reassured him that any man that comes into our lives would be all of those.

Within a year I met my husband and he and I had this conversation. My husband loved basketball and children. He was serving as a youth pastor in his church when we met, so I could clearly see that he was great with children. We met on an online dating site. due to me working so much that I didn't have the time to meet anyone outside of that. We instantly clicked, but there was no meeting my children until I knew that he was good enough. We spent a lot of time on the phone because he was from another state, we met up halfway between each other a few times because

I wanted to sniff him out. After a few months, he met the children and they instantly fell in love with him! He was working overtime to make sure they were comfortable. I asked him one time what he would do if my kids didn't like him and his reply was "work harder". He worked hard and my children enjoyed seeing me happy and spending time with James. We did fun activities to create memories together; James and I spent time continuing to get to know one another. He accepted the fact that I was a divorcee, a breast cancer survivor, that I loved God,(he loved that part the most), that I was a mother of two wonderful children, worked a crazy job and had dreams. We met in April and byDecember were engaged. Less than one year later we had the twins. God had not only blessed me with an amazing husband but he doubled our family!

I grew up with step parents and it was very tough to see someone in place of my biological parent. My children loved James and what we were becoming, because it happened at a pace that allowed them to heal from my divorce. They expressed to me when they were ready, and we moved forward together. They understand that James is no replacement of their father, but they are very blessed to have two men that love and care for them dearly.

After the breast cancer, I had to get used to the new me. My brain works differently and things that I could do with no problem take a little more study and thought now. I still have my moments where I cry because the effects of cancer don't end when they say it's been removed. I give back when I can when it comes to that aspect. I speak publicly about my experience, and do my best to express to any young women (or man) to know their bodies and do what's necessary to keep themselves healthy. There is healing in helping others from something that once caused you so much pain.

For Our Daughters Inc, is growing each year. We take pride in helping young women advocate for themselves, because this means a longer, healthier life for each of them. I work very hard at not only growing the organization, but growing myself as a leader.

This book is huge step for me. Telling my story is allowing me to experience the freedom that comes with being comfortable advocating for yourself. The vision is for For Our Daughters Inc. to be international and we will get there one step at a time!

My relationship with both of my parents is better. My father and I get together on a regular basis to hang out and chat. My children love their time with their grandfather. I get to see him be the man that I remember when I was a kid with my own children and it's amazing. I enjoy our talks and getting advice from my father. He texts me every morning with "GM", and just about every morning I get them my heart smiles. I love sitting and listening to him talk about his dreams as a young man, because I have the same tenacity and dreams that he used to have. God has truly restored what was taken away from me as a young woman, and for that I am grateful. I look forward to birthday parties for the kids with him or just his occasional Sunday dinners, he's a pretty cool man! My sister has one daughter. My niece and daughter are the best of friends. My sister and I, on the other hand, fight like we are still kids. We then make up just to fight again. I love my little sister with all of my heart and she loves me. We share our life stories, and every so often get to talk about how happy we are that we were blessed with one another. We make it a priority that our girls grow up together and that means the world to me. Every time my niece comes over I sit and listen to them talk and laugh. I'm grateful to God for the restoration of our family, it enhances our futures (our children).

My mother and I now have a very transparent relationship. She's not a very emotional woman so giving her kisses and such make her uneasy, which means I do it more (just to get under her skin). We are at a point where we are open to talking about issues with one another when we have them, and then we move on! Sometimes when I yell at my kids I hear my mother, and have to call her laughing. I call her for her food recipes during the holidays, she is a great cook! I don't claim perfection in our relationship because there is no such thing, but I do claim a willingness to work at love. At the end of the day love is something that we all crave.

The aunt and uncle that took me in when I was 15 years old are still the joys of my life. I can still call on my aunt anytime of the day or night and my uncle still makes sure to tell me how proud of me he is. They keep up with what I have going on as if I was one of their own children, and I appreciate that. I am forever grateful to them for their role in saving my life; I try to tell and show them that every chance I get.

I have friends that were there for me throughout my cancer journey that mean the world to me. The circle of friends that I am blessed to have, we inspire and sharpen one another. To have people in my life that can fully understand that we are all valuable is priceless! We are fully aware and understand that friendship is a two-way street, and we encourage and love one another unconditionally.

When I changed my view of why God allowed me to go through the tough times that I endured, I suddenly realized that the heavier the trial was, the wider my reach would be. What you go through is never just for you. It's for the glory of God!Mercedes Wilson

12

THIS ONE IS ABOUT YOU!

I don't claim, nor do I want to act as though I know everything. I can't share my life with you and not end this book without a chapter about God, his sovereignty, and the twinkle that he has in his eyes for you!

I have to start at the cross and what that signifies for us. There is no way that I would sacrifice my child for anyone else. I have a difficult enough time missing a part of one of their basketball games for any other event. To sacrifice something that means everything to him to gain us is what God did when he sent Jesus. John 3:16;AMP is more than a mantra to me. The scripture reads: For God so [greatly] loved *and* dearly prized the world, that He [even] gave His [One and] only begotten Son, so that whoever believes *and* trusts in Him [as Savior] shall not perish, but have eternal life.

Think about it, you were worth so much to God that he gave his son to be connected to you. Can you imagine the desperation to be in someone's presence you would have to experience to give your only child? I think about that when I go periods of time without praying. He created an open-door policy for me to come to him, with no restrictions, and I take that for granted at times! He wants to commune with us.

You are the apple of his eye

The apple of the eye is the globe of the center of the eye. God is very protective over us, look up part of a scripture in *Zechariah 2:8;KJV ... for he that toucheth you toucheth the apple of his eye.*

Please know that when you are going through things that are tough, God is with you. When you think of being the apple of someone else's eye, you think that life is going to be grand and you will have no troubles. With God it's the opposite. He sees your potential, after all he created you, and wants to pull out of you what is needed for you to fulfill your calling. The trials that you endure are clues into what you have in the future; grab ahold of them, learn, grow, and soar! He loves us enough to not leave us where we are.

Your walls are continually before God

Isaiah 49:16;KJV *"Behold, I have graven thee upon the palms of my hands; thy walls are continually before me"*. God is telling us that our walls, no matter what they are, he sees them. There is no place that you can go that we can't welcome God into our life situations. He loves us enough that he has put us on the palms of his hand.

There is never a time that you are experiencing hardships and God is not there overseeing it. So many ask the question "if God is really there, why isn't he stopping all of the bad things?" I have asked that question many times, and the one thing that I can say is that we all have choices. Just like we make choices, we deal with the consequences of those choices. It doesn't reflect God's lack of goodness and mercy when we go through things, but rather his strength working through us when we make it and can then give testament to his love. The bible says that God teaches us while keeping his eyes on us in Psalms 32:8:KJV *"I will instruct you and teach you in the way which you should go; I will counsel you with My eye upon you."*

God tells us right from the beginning, we will suffer trials, but he has us! How many folks can guarantee that at any point of life when things get tough that they will always have you? None!

There's nothing that can separate you from Him

I don't care what anyone tells you, there is nothing that can separate you from God. Paul said it so well in *Romans 8:38-39;KJV when he said: "For I am persuaded, that neither death, nor life, nor angels, nor principalities, nor powers, nor things present, nor things to come,*
Nor height, nor depth, nor any other creature, shall be able to separate us from the love of God, which is in Christ Jesus our Lord."
God sacrificed His son to bring us together for eternity, there is nothing that we can do that will negate Jesus' blood! God gave us the power of choice, but also put in a barrier between us and hell, and that barrier is Jesus. So, in our failures, intentional or unintentional, we can always make our way back home through the blood. True repentance always ends up with your sins at the cross, please remember that! As long as you have the word of God forever before you, your best days are still ahead of you. I can guarantee that!

With God on your side, you can't lose! You got this!

Don't complicate prayer

I love prayer and worship. Prayer is what gets me through life. Simply put, it's a two-way conversation with God where you talk AND listen. I am giving an example of a simple prayer that I pray, and hopefully it helps you. I am adding this because for too many of us, prayer is this mysterious thing, when really, God is just waiting for us to say something. Try it! It will change your life. Start small if you need to, but just START.

I love my husband, children, family, friends, jobs, etc. BUT there is only one place that I can go and have complete peace. This place will never be matched and I never leave feeling void. My soul finds rest and my mind gains peace. I get strength, direction, wisdom, and get to see what true love looks like. The only place that I can go and learn what Mercedes is truly about is when I go down on my knees in prayer.

It's in my prayer time that I get direction for my life. Just like communication is a two-way street with those around you, it's the same thing with God. God enjoys talking with us. The bible says in 1 Thessalonians 5:16-18(KJV) to rejoice evermore. Pray without ceasing. In every thing give thanks: for this is the will of God in Christ Jesus concerning you.

Prayer is how God gives you insight on the plans for your future, for your family, friends, and business moves. It is in prayer that God gives me insight on how to love my husband, areas to pray for my children, how to be a blessing to someone that may be hurting, and most importantly, God's love for me.

God shows me different parts of my life in prayer, and that is how I make my next group of decisions. If it doesn't line up with what I was told, I don't do it! We live in a fast-paced world,

and that can make it easy for us to get lost in the shuffle. Prayer slows me down and helps me stay focused.

One thing that I can promise you, if you give prayer a try and make it up in your mind to not only talk but listen, it will change your life!

A sample prayer of mine:

Thank you for sending your son Jesus to die for my sins. Thank you for creating a way for me to always be able to come to you, for being able to hear from you. Holy Spirit use me today. Give me wisdom, the right words to say, to know when to keep my mouth shut, and how to deal with my children. Thank you for being who you are in my life. Thank you for my family, friends, children, husband, and job. Thank you for turning things around for my good. Forgive me for being anything outside of what you made me to be. I am so grateful that I made it! Use what I have been through for your glory, to set people free, to show someone that they are not alone. Help me to be a light today, to help someone, to show them your love, to be the salt of the earth. Lead me to those that may be sad today, those that are hurting and need a smile, those that may be confused and just need a touch from you. When others see me, I want them to see you. Help me to see things from an aerial view, I want to see the big picture.

Cover my family and friends. Cover those that are hurting around the world. Stop the plans of the enemy today in our country, protect your people, bring families back together, comfort those that may have lost a loved one today. Be their peace in the storm.

Cover our children. Give me wisdom on how to raise mine while showing them how to be a light in their affairs of life. Protect them while at school. Cover my husband. Give him favor on his job and help him to bless those around him wherever he goes. I thank you for blessing me with him and I ask that you continue to bring us closer together for your glory. Help us to be examples for our children in all that we do. Speak to him today, we all need you. Prepare us for what is to come, in the name of Jesus I pray Amen.

Scriptures used:

Romans 5:3-4;KJV
Proverbs 13:12;AMP
Deuteronomy 30:3;AMP
Matthew 11:28;AMP

Psalm 27:10;AMP
Ephesians 4:26;AMP
Proverbs 31:10;AMP
Philippians 4:19;AMP

Isaiah 49:2;AMP
Luke 6:45;AMP.
Matthew 17:20;AMP
Proverbs 13:3 AMP

Philippians 4:8
2 corinthians 10:5
Proverbs 18:16;AMP

John 1:8;KJV

proverbs 19:17;KJV
Proverbs 3:27;KJV
1 Corinthians 13:1-7;KJV
James 3:17;KJV

Proverbs 11:14;KJV
Proverbs 25:8;KJV
John 3:16;AMP
Zechariah 2:8;KJV

Isaiah 49:16;KJV
Psalms 32:8;KJV
Romans 8:38-39;KJV
1 Thessalonians 5:16-18(KJV)

Books that I read that really impacted me:

THE MANTLE OF ESTHER (Discovering the Power of Intercession) by Larry Christenson

WHEN IT ALL FALLS APART(Finding Healing, Joy, and Victory Through the Pain) by Riva Tims

LIES AT THE ALTER (The Truth About Great Marriages) by Dr. Robin Smith

BATTLEFIELD of the mind(Winning the Battle in Your Mind) by Joyce Meyer

I AM VICTORY(Kingdom Principles To A Victorious Life) by Victory Vernon

THE LADY, HER LOVER, AND LORD by Bishop T.D. Jakes

NOTES

My family and I

Photo Credit: Joed Viera

My husband and I

Photo credit: Yvonne Gan Photography

My father and I

Photo Credit:Ally Spongr

For Our Daughters Incorporated

Photo Credit: Ally Spongr

UPFRONT

October 2017

For Our Daughters Incorporated

Mercedes Wilson
Founder and Executive Director

Cover of Upfront Magazine 2017

Photo Credit: Ally Spongr

SPECIAL CANCER SURVIVOR ISSUE

Daily Buzz 7/5

TOPICAL TALK ⟬ BUFFALO STYLE

Description is DailyBuzz 716 Show
Photo Credit: Joe Maulucci

Buffalo

Healthy

October 2012

FREE

Living

"FOR OUR DAUGHTERS"
KNOW THE SIGNS OF BREAST CANCER

FIBBING ABOUT
FIBER

ELIMINATING THE
EMPTY NEST
BLUES

Photo by James Haschmann

www.BuffaloHealthyLiving.com

VISIT THE AUTHORS WEBSITE:
MERCEDESEWILSON.COM

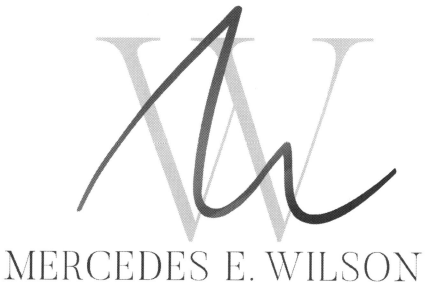

MERCEDES E. WILSON

Cover photo: Ally Spongr
Cover outfit: YMG CUSTOM APPAREL AND MORE

Printed in the United States
By Bookmasters